T0119707

BEYOND *the* REACH

BEYOND *the* REACH

P O E M S

Deborah Cummins

BkMk Press
University of Missouri-Kansas City

Copyright © 2002 Deborah Cummins.
All rights reserved.

BkMk Press
University of Missouri-Kansas City
5101 Rockhill Road
Kansas City, Missouri 64110
(816) 235-2558 (voice)
(816) 235-2611 (fax)
bkmk@umkc.edu
www.umkc.edu/bkmk

MAC
MISSOURI ARTS COUNCIL

Financial assistance for this book has been provided by the Missouri
Arts Council, as state agency.

Cover art: *Woman on Porch* (1958) by Richard Diebenkorn
Art reproduced with permission of New Orleans Museum of Art
(Museum purchase through National Endowment for the Arts
Matching Grant) and the Estate of Richard Diebenkorn
Book Design: Susan L. Schurman; Managing Editor: Ben Furnish

Special thanks to Michelle Boisseau and Michael Nelson
Thanks also to Jessica Hylan, Jeri Keimeg, John Bullard, Jennifer Ickes

Library of Congress Cataloging-in-Publication Data

Cummins, Deborah, 1949-
    Beyond the reach: poems / Deborah Cummins.
        p. cm.
    ISBN 1-886157-38-3 (pbk.)
    I. Title.
    PS3603.U66 B49 2002
    811'.6--dc21
                                        2002007229

Second printing: 2005

Acknowledgments

I wish to extend acknowledgment to the editors of the following publications where some of these poems previously appeared, a few in somewhat different versions:

Cimarron Review: "By Choice"
Crab Orchard Review: "Last Week a Million Butterflies"
     (as "Hostages to Shine") and "Walking the Dog"
     (as "Opossum")
The Gettysburg Review: "To the Days Lost in August"
     and "From a Dune above Herring Cove Beach"
Gulf Coast: "The Bisbee Donkeys"
Laurel Review: "Refusal" and "Elegy for J."
The Nebraska Review: "Passage"
New England Review: "In the Hospital"
Orion: "What the Body Remembers" and "From Away"
Petroglyph: "Mercy"
Poetry Daily: "In the Hospital" and "Just When"
Shenandoah: "My Mind's Eye Opens Before the Light Gets Up"
Tar River Poetry: "A House-Moving," "Attempting a Prayer,"
     "At Ames Pond," "Jeremy Point," "Just When" and
     "Salt Marsh"
Third Coast: "To Get a Closer Look"

"In the White Mountains" (as "In the White Mountains, Trying
     to Describe Autumn"), "Marital Agreement," and
     "Relics" first appeared in a chapbook, *From The Road It
     Looks Like Paradise* (State Street Press, 1997).

"The Bisbee Donkeys" is anthologized in *And We The
     Creatures*, Dream Horse Press, 2002

"Last Week a Million Butterflies" (as "Hostages to Shine") received a 1999 Illinois Arts Council Literary Award.

I am deeply grateful to Andrea Hollander Budy for her valuable insights, her close reading of this manuscript and, most especially, her friendship. Thanks, too, to Stephen Dunn, Kathleen Lynch and Robert Alexander who helped shape some of these poems. Gratitude is also due editors Peter Makuck, Bill Trowbridge, Judith Kitchen and Allison Joseph for publishing some of my first poems.

I owe much appreciation to the Illinois Arts Council for various fellowships and awards and to the MacDowell Colony, Yaddo, the Ragdale Foundation and the Virginia Center for the Creative Arts where many of these poems were written.

For their sustaining love, support and encouragement, I thank my family, especially Bob. And finally, a nod must go to beloved Ben whose daily companionship makes the journey sweeter.

Contents

III. Meanwhile

For Bob, always—

and in memory of James Wilton Grigsby, 1940-2002

I

Passage

In the White Mountains

All these trees and leaves, and each bears
no resemblance to any other. I'd have to describe
each one. And because the wind gusts up or the sun
disappears behind a cloud, I'd need to update
every description by the minute, a task
harder than Monet's. Then there's the matter
of imperceptible decay, of obsolescence, winter
due to arrive any second.

Perhaps if I stayed with color,
the yellows and oranges, the russets,
occasional purples, and, of course, the greens,
the partly greens, greens closer to yellow,
a full spectrum of hue, all manners of comparisons possible:
to gourds and squashes, citrus and grain,
to flame and flowers, stars I've yet to learn to name.
And naming the colors — *ochre, cadmium, citron, chrome* —
might make it more specific, might arrest,
for an instant, autumn's dazzling passage.

As if that's what I'm after: language's momentary stasis.
As if the adjectives for leaves I labor with —
dappled, mottled, marbled, splotched — might keep
this gold-disked birch from squandering all its currency.
It's not enough: reaching into the jeweler's bag,
stretching for the anvil of the metalsmith,

all those *pavés*, mosaics, and *cloisonnés* to capture
this luminosity, this voracious clarity
of unnameable golden light.

On this white escarpment I've dragged
my shadow to, at this confluence of yellow mountain
and blue inveterate sky, against this elaborate dialogue
where no boundaries blur, and nothing obfuscates
to what end beneath their golden splendor these trees will come,
I recognize this attempt at description
as elegy, lament.
But nothing dying needs to be so lavish.
Nothing dying needs such fire.
It's the living I stand before, this ferocious burning.

In the Hospital

Now, his appetite lost, too, he wants
to hear about food, memorable meals:
grilled squab on simmered fennel,
a velvety bisque of butternut squash,
wild boar ragouted with Norcia truffle,
the marriage of Stilton and walnut.

He makes his partner reconstruct in words
a forty-garlic chicken, the one-hundred corners
of nine-spice dumplings. They shake their heads
at the cruelty of one thousand-year-old eggs,
find the humor in a *potage à la tête de veau*
mistakenly ordered one summer in Dijon.

Machines against the back wall whir.
Bubbles rise in several tubes. At the window,
the sun, right on schedule, checks in,
carries him back to his mother's kitchen,
the sliced cucumbers that glistened
in a blue glass bowl. After diagnosis

she fed him on paper plates, and still hesitates
kissing him on the mouth. His partner,
trying to trick the body into another remission,
returns them to Crete and a slaughtered lamb
spitting into the fire, recalls in great particularity

an aspic's trembling transparency.

In the hall, nurses go on perfecting
their zip and bustle, specialists huddle
over their charted percentages, odds.
Options waning, as if to feed some final hunger,
Tuscany gets mentioned: a field
stitched with vines, silvered with olive. On the horizon,

a walled city assembled from stones and dust,
nine churches tolling out hours, one by one.
The simplest *al fresco* lunch: bread, wine,
a clean white cloth, each scintillant fold
that in a rinse of light, touched by the kindest breeze,
seemed capable, almost, of rising.

A House-Moving

Summer folks, locals, we've all come to gawk
at a white, two-story clapboard
rolling through town, its ponderous weight
that of celebrity. The owners
have inherited a better view of the cove
and for such an undertaking, there's a surprising
absence of shuddering, clanking.
As if, rooted to its foundation 120 years,
its accumulations more intricate than the tides',
this house is going agreeably, the sway
of curtains at its open windows almost a wave.

Tomorrow, its owners will awake
in their familiar beds, retrieve from accustomed places
toothbrushes, cups. They'll see the water
at a different angle, more light will crown
some taller spruce, Gene Eaton's pickup
will grind through the gears from a greater distance
and they might believe
it is in their power to move the world.
A momentary lapse like my wish for a Hereafter
where little is changed. A simple awakening:
the table already set, my favorite goblets gleaming.

Attempting a Prayer

Outside her window, clouds are fixed
like sentries at a gate. If only she could
get a glimpse. If only it weren't so one-sided.
She opens her mouth but vowels are caught
in her throat: the You, the I.
She can't remember if she's supposed to kneel.
She doesn't know what signs to make, or look for.
A limb unhinges a leaf. It falls without sound.
Pine needles lie on the lawn, rusted and useless.
Dust collects on the sill. And how
the lake refuses to stay still, goes on
slapping the sand, the rocks that seem to swell
with their importance. Why can't she at least
be grateful for the sun through trees?
Why can't she get the words out? If nothing else,
the abstract words by which she thinks she lives—
duty, say, or *belief*? *Malignancy*
she's had to learn to spell. Inconsequential
when reduced to letters, a few
errant cells. This morning, her face
in the mirror was almost recognizable,
her hair, growing back, nearly natural.
The world could've been made of more
comprehensible happinesses:
her husband reading a book in the next room,
the dog asleep on the couch.

If only the larkspur by the fenceline
weren't that shade of cobalt,
the lindens such an extravagant green.

Mercy

From the hospital's windowless room, my father
can't point at the world's inhuman beauty.
He can't piss in a tube,
is as speechless as an animal.
There's so little I can do for him:
rub his feet, hold his hands, go on
noticing cedar waxwing, yellow-throated vireo,
try to bring him the world alive in words.

No matter what he said about mercy
when I was nine, I didn't understand
why a bullet was necessary for the horse
whose only mistake was to step into a hole,
or why after, when we drove to Flint Creek to swim,
he insisted on our total immersion.

Helping him over is language meant to spare me.
Pulling the plug are words I still refuse.
In this windowless room, I try
to tell him about an indigo bunting
with its tangible throat and wings,
but all the while I'm thinking ahead
to *It's over*.

The horse thudded to the ground
like a felled tree and slowly thrashed. An image

it's taken years for me to comprehend—
those legs never again had to bear
the weight of being strong.

The Bisbee Donkeys

Lowered in by pulleys and belts,
donkeys were once used in the
Bisbee Mine to haul carts of ore.
Some lived as long as seventeen
years in the mine. Most went blind.

Going down, they must've kicked,
fighting for a last breath of real air, a final
glimpse of light. Below,
they must've stumbled over iron-rutted tracks
until darkness thickened, shadows disappeared.

Here I should remind myself
animals don't reason, can't differentiate
between justice and fate,
have no knowledge of dust,
how it packs lungs, smothers desire.

They have no memories
of wet, green grass. Still,
beneath bright planets, a dispassionate moon,
if only for an afternoon, an occasional night,
the miners could've hauled the donkeys out.

And here, I could change the story,
write that they did. But I prefer to think
of those men as incapable

of such cruelty. They wouldn't haul
the donkeys out, only to drag them back,

considering, especially, the newest arrivals
who knew only a mother's shaggy flanks,
her black milk, born
into the palpable pitch
out of whatever instincts that, even if hobbled,

nevertheless break free.
How blinding all that sudden light would be,
the unfathomable blue.
A kindness then. By the men
who day after day had to coldly

ratchet themselves down, descend,
stygian, with shovel and axe,
the pinpricks of their lanterned miners' hats
a constellated sky brought underground:
distant celestial animals, fixed, wheeling.

What the Body Remembers

The body remembers
on moonless nights, in a certain laughter,
whenever the drawn bow of a cello
or the pianissimo of keys and pedals
crosses from one realm to another.
The body remembers
long after the descent into fever.
After the car has spun
to rest on the crusty river.
Or after the man over you, your arms pinned,
at last stops slapping.
Some mornings, on waking,
what the body knows falls into sight
as light condenses around pulled shades.
Until what's quietly familiar –
the dresser, an open book – comes back
in hard and certain outline.

And now here, at the trail's edge,
sunlight through trees
illuminates the vixen's body.
Her alert, cock-eared silence
spells a definitive *no*. What pose of mine
would explain *I mean no harm?*
One of her kits inches forward.
All instinct, it retreats.

The vixen, from a distance, can only look.
To her, I'm something other
than foul weather on the horizon.
If she could pray,
it would be for a creature less threatening.
There's no way to tell her
I know that helplessness.
How it's contained in the body.
How it doesn't leave.

Northern Flicker

after Thomas Lynch

It died with its eyes open,
this one I look into
a mirror that no longer reflects,
a door ajar to an empty room.
There's no hint
of surprise at what, mid-flight,
claimed this flicker's life,
nor what, before a final breath,
it might have seen.

How similar a human corpse's
open eyes. No clue
of eternal light or black abyss,
of whatever, in their new sight,
is there, or is not. No wonder
coins are pressed on lids. Or a missal
wedged between chest and chin.
As though the dead may try to tell
what they now know
and the living don't.

I should leave this flicker
in the dropped needles and moss
but I'll uncrook the bent wings,

bury it, as if compelled
by customs of bereavement,
of rare wood coffins, rosary-
laced fingers, corpses
made ready, even though,
as the eyes show, the body is
no longer relevant.

Passage

Once more, in their dumb unknowing,
sandhill cranes are pulled to a place
they must again and again get back to.
I lean on a rake and scan the sky
for their small Chinese brush strokes arrowing blue.
But it's their wild, wondrous sound
that pierces me, their high trill
more thrilling than two young deer that at dawn
incised our lawn with their slender hooves,
lured by the dwarf apples' windfall.

Wherever the cranes' journey ends,
some shoreline probed by assiduous tides,
my garden's just another particular
and less important than the prairies, hills
or rivers the cranes clamor over,
all breath and bellow and creaking pinions,
their passage as compelled and unyielding
as the thump a ripe apple makes
falling. And quick
as that sound, the cranes are here, then not.
I'm left with dirt and rake.

As a child, I lay awake
in the colorless dark and waited for dawn's oncoming
freight, its whistle's single mournful whine.

How that last reverberating note,
especially when it was cold, hung
in the air of my room, our house,
above the river thick with ice, the hills beyond.
I didn't understand but knew.
Not the sound, but the ache of after.

By Choice

In the garden, my sister's child plays
with collapsing flowers, annuals
he's already outlived.
He addresses each browned head by name:
Dee. Dee. The same syllable he uses
for birds, cats, anything pointed at:
the pin oak baring its bones,
the grasshopper rising
into the end of her journey.
He speaks a language all his own.
In his lexicon, no should-haves,
no might-have-beens.
This morning at my desk, I misread
fear of cessation as failed succession
and now on my knees with this season's bulbs,
I think *bury* instead of *plant*. As if it's regret
I'm putting in the ground, not something bright
as tulip, as promise. Beneath sunlight
sifting through trees like scattered seeds,
my nephew holds up handfuls of earth
as if each particle were holy,
scratches with a stick in the dirt.
It's easy to forget there's history yet to be made.
Or that, instead of June, the garden all gloating green,
it's October and I still don't wish
he were mine.

To the Days Lost in August

Summer is over on the island.
Pleasure boats are cradled.
The schooner that hauled tourists
to the archipelagoes
is dry-docked in Camden.
Neva's has closed for the season,
the *New York Times* gone back
to the mainland. At Fisherman's Friend,
lobster by the pound is off the menu.
No one picnics on Caterpillar Hill.

Summer is over on the island.
Orion's retreated higher.
Fog, thickening, salty, closes in.
Birches are past their yellow,
maples their red. Winds
back around Northeast,
argue with hemlocks,
petition the hackmatacks.
Acorns become brisk business
in the leaves, needles. Winesaps,
thick with bees, distill.

Any morning, a first frost
will glaze the cabbages,
chicory, and aster, the salt hay

not baled in silos.
Squalls will flood the pilings.
No boats, for days, will put off.
The talk over mended traps and rakes
has turned to tarpon, marlin,
to the days lost in August.
Hopes for revision, a few
rekindling days out of season, dwindle.
The sky ebbs into gray,
darker than the water,
darker than the woodstove's spirals.

From Away

after Elizabeth Bishop

Think of the storm roaming the sky uneasily,
of how evening enters afternoon.
Listen to it growl.

Think how they must look now: the islands
thick with spruce, a few Impressionist birches,
how they pitch and sway

and where, on the indifferent rocks worked with lichen,
sooty cormorants crank in their wings, a Giacometti heron
abandons its stilted watch.

Think of the harbor, the chilly singing in the halyards,
trawlers returning like obedient retrievers,
how lightning makes the water shine.

The rain there pelts the barnacled shoreward pilings,
the small red buildings, Main Street's roses, lupines.
The rivalry of sea and sky is unquellable, ancient.

Now, perhaps, the storm veers inland
away from the fish shacks, the bearded weirs,
away from St. Brendan the Navigator's canted steeple.

Think how, beyond a line of squalls,

the single boat that didn't make it back pulls

a skirt of gulls, its incantatory diesel thumping.

At Ames Pond

In the reedy edges, a heron
picks its way slowly, ignorant
of this black polished water,
these small noiseless explosions,
lilies rising on their pale poles.
The heron can't consider
the pond's unstoppable decay
or how, not so far away, the world
assembles important troubles.
Likewise, a fish, splashing upward
like a quick silver flower,
pursues whatever fills its belly.
I don't envy the heron, the wordless fish,
this granite boulder's rock-ness.
I don't wish to be so woven
into the fabric that I can't stand
upright, apart, and ably witness.
I'd never give up
my opposable thumbs or my lips,
aware, with my kind,
of how to use them. I wouldn't swap
the burden of grief
for protective coloration, old hurts
for the sting of nettle, wasp. I want
to be able to fool with fire,
name the aches, understand the world

is an indifferent place.
With the pace of an hour's hand,
the heron lifts one leg.
Pink lilies blossom
without a single want.
How, with no rush
toward oblivion, it goes on and on.

II

Relics

Punching the Air

The summer I began to bleed,
nearly every day a neighbor kid
chased my younger brother until I became
a boy again and pinned the kid to the gravel.
From her porch, Mrs. DeGroot insisted
I come to her that instant.
Dutiful, I marched into her house
where nights after supper, as the rest of us played,
her husband held his children
captive around the Bible.
In her kitchen, I chafed at the gleaming counters,
a spotless sink, the stink of Ajax.
Clouds scudded past
curtains embroidered with windmills
as she explained "rough-necking wasn't proper"
for a young woman. Her rolled up sleeves
barely concealed bright fleshy bruises.

Months later, after they'd swabbed
their breakfast nooks, pinned up laundry,
my mother's friends circled our table to talk,
drink coffee, something else grown women did,
and one of them said Ed DeGroot's death,
how he'd been crushed beneath a loaded truck,
was fit punishment for a man who beat his wife.
But what of her, a woman compliant

beneath him all those years? Or the skinny sons
to whom he'd shown how it was done,
who liked to watch me on the lawn
practicing cartwheels, splits, punching
the air with my fists and shredded pom-poms.

To Get a Closer Look

Saturdays, after funeral Mass, I scavenged pews
searching for gold-rimmed holy cards of haloed saints.
In the Latin I couldn't read,
they commemorated with dates and small prayers
our parish's recent dead. Who they were didn't matter.

Old Mrs. Alekna collected them all.
I climbed three flights with my loot,
endured her musty flat, her sour breath,
the cat that pissed in a corner,
anything to get a closer look at her bristly goiter.

Already the size of an orange,
each week, to my eyes, it grew larger.
She couldn't button her collars,
couldn't straighten her head beneath the lamp
where she studied each card, arranged them,

after Jesus with his bleeding heart,
after his Immaculate Mother,
into a precise descending order:
Joseph wielding his awl, Sebastian pierced with arrows,
headless Agnes, Agatha with her breasts on a platter.

When I couldn't look any longer, couldn't resist
putting my hand to my own neck to check

for menacing bumps, I took in her silent Victrola,
the cabbage roses fading up her wall, afternoon darkness
gathering in shapeless pools. I felt blessed

she wasn't my aunt or grandmother
whom I might've been forced to kiss.
But when my hunger for cards
turned to Nellie Fox, Mickey Mantle,
passports to the boys and their wild wondrous smells,

I thought less and less of Mrs. Alekna in her faded dress,
in her body where for years nothing happened
except a ghoulish division of cells.
I gave up believing
she might be a suffering-in-silence saint.

No shaft of light had ever careened
through her window. No ecstatic look
consumed her face. Even the clean, starched nuns
went out, wore veils and long dresses,
were married, at least, to God.

At Cody, Barnes & Wentworth

Once I had an office here, too,
among these men in silk ties, Italian suits.
I was the exception,
not to be confused with the exceptional.
After all this time, I'd like to be forgiven

for not noticing the other women
who left behind their confused children,
their dirty houses, neglected gardens,
to weave between the Xerox and In/Out baskets
delivering coffee, hauling lunches into board rooms.

From my office I billed clients, a way to measure
what in the last hour I'd paid for:
dinner at Bigg's, mixed doubles at Saddle & Cycle.
What could I have loved here?
What was so potent?

How many smiles did I have to brandish
at male colleagues I wanted to spend
no more than five minutes of my life with?
It was supposed to be touchless,
except on crowded elevators, the brushed against

shoulders, elbows. Eyes
should have traveled only to faces.

The view from the 40th floor still stuns,
until, like the ghost ache of a limb
no longer there, I remember

the eight hours daily severed.
And oh, how I still understand what is expected
as the man I've come to see greets me,
and reaching for his hand, I summon
my old voice from bedroom to office.

After the Affair

Weeks of unusual warmth
have brought on tulips, assorted jonquils,
but now, breaking all promise,
it's snowing, and robins, newly arrived,
respond with their single three-note song.
They can't vary the melody,
can't alter their tone to suggest
anger at being deceived.
The robins don't confess their mistake
with anything other than cheerful music,
don't betray any wish to possess
exotic plumage, or like the roseate spoonbill,
the glossy ibis, to live full-time in the tropics.

Common grackles are more honest.
Those afternoons last fall, huge flocks gathered
across town, on the other side
of drawn drapes, a bolted door,
my clothes dropped over a chair.
They made no music.
Their cries were loud, raucous
until, having enough of their nuisance,
a man next door fired pellets
into the pines and shedding maples.
Like so many good intentions,
the panicked grackles vanished.

The smallest branches, unweighted, shivered.
I could've told the man it was futile,
that such birds would be back to scavenge
whatever from the leaves and needles had fallen.

Marital Agreement

To win back those afternoons in bed, I sprawl
across ours and imagine him, not you.
In that upstairs room, in that borrowed house
foreign enough to heighten everything.
The way I remember it: not a false move,
all effortless expertise
patinaed not with practice or time,
but unthinking passion like spontaneous crime.
I wish I could say it was a place I'd never been,
an historical moment remembered now,
out of necessity, incorrectly.
For example, I could so easily recall
an ashtray balanced on my belly,
blue ribbons of smoke snaking toward the ceiling
though neither he nor I touched cigarettes.
But the empty bottle of Margaux
on the bureau was fact. And the act
of shadows lengthening on the wall
in spite of my willing the sun not to slip.
Nothing else, those afternoons, took such working at.
On this bed where I lie now, nothing rocks.
Nothing in this room tries to prevent
the sun from going down, from dropping
like a lid on a box. In that other room,
when the darkness came, he and I lit a candle
and watched a moth seek again and again the flame,

willing, or was it longing, to be consumed.
From the bottom of the stairs, you at last
call up. You wonder aloud what am I doing,
then wait, without climbing, to find out.
We already know in whatever I answer
there'll be enough truth to satisfy us.
Until next time, when it's your turn
to look away, and to my questions answer,
"Nothing," or perhaps, "Nowhere,"
and I won't, believe me, believe you.

Old Hurts

Before we have time to mulch the yard,
a hard freeze forces us in, instructs us
to huddle. We aren't prepared,
aren't past old hurts we worked to avoid all summer
with golf, tennis, separate walks on the beach.
We need blankets and sweaters from the cedar chest
but we shiver in cotton, linen, jack up the heat,
abandon the language of touch,
speak incidentally, try to be graceful, even kind.
But it isn't kindness that drives us to withdraw
into different rooms, ignoring the long dark season,
its limited number of hours to sleep, old movies to rent.
Only so many pots of soup require frequent stirring—

bisques, rich cream reductions,
small portions for delicate appetites.
We need ragout, a stew, something thick
with onions and garlic, that can simmer for hours,
doesn't require much tending.
Or no, stir fry, cooked fast, high heat, oil spattering
in small beads like water on skin after a swim.
Or make it Mexican, lots of poblanos,
so many chiles we begin to sweat,
have to strip for a shower. Or what if
we fix nothing and the cabinets empty
to a last crust of bread we'll have to tear in two.
And then just salt, bitter salt.

Refusal

And the angel Gabriel said:
"The Holy Ghost shall come
upon thee...that holy thing
which shall be born of thee
shall be called the Son of God."
 —Luke 1:36

What if Mary, young wife of Joseph, had been able
to refuse, if she ate of disobedience's bittersweet fruit –
pain, labor, dust in the grave—
and was linked navel to navel with Eve?
Let's say she considered her husband, as I might mine,
finding with his lips the insides
of her elbows, the backs of her knees,
her breasts and belly. Think of the children
they'd have been free to beget!
If Mary had been able to refuse, her face
wouldn't appear in paintings, icons, or frescoes.
One day, Caravaggio would ask Lena
to climb the scaffold in Piazza Navone
and depict some other chosen woman, not Mary,
who, though blessed, nevertheless
would often feel inexplicable sadness,
like the kind just after sex.
Let's imagine, after flying back
into her imperfect body as if on heavy wings,
she'd find there again an undeniable hunger.

Sunday Morning, Late August

She's never sat at a steamy café near Pont Neuf
and fed a lover a perfect *tarte tatin*,
never slept naked in a rented room
on Place de la Madeleine, shutters open to the rain.
Already, a thousand times before this morning,
she's wished to be someplace else if only
a little further down the beach.

In this small town on the Cape, even clouds
drag away their important business.
Flimsy chairs face seaward, as if in wait
for something glorious, drastic.
An ocean away from Boulevard St. Germain,
the water shimmers like unspooled foil.
Some other life lies elsewhere:

hers, unclaimed.
But why, now, as her husband crosses the yard
and with customary gestures plucks —
oh, how banal — a common daisy,
does her blood, running its old familiar route,
deliver such bounty to her heart?

Last Week a Million Butterflies

*"... a butterfly stirring the air in Peking can
transform storm systems next month in New York."*
                                    —*James Gleick*

Last week a million butterflies rose up from southern Mexico.
Which has something or nothing to do with the flames
devouring Yosemite, the smoke that half a continent away
is behind the particulate brilliance
of this sunset here tonight. I don't want to believe
that at the other end of such radiance is fire.
That the butterflies traveling their ancient paths
might well be headed in that direction,
mistaking the burning light ahead for the usual sun.
As, too, a flock of birds might.
Or the man I love, making his way home on a plane,
who might glance up from his book, think
it's only sunlight ravishing a lake.
Hostages to shine, the butterflies
will keep on coming, wave after wave
of powdered parchment, mysterious feelers.
I can't say what part they may have played in it:
the thunderstorm's first spark, the lick of flame,
this fiery orange that insists on this particular glass pane.
Or if there's a connection between the next leaf to drop
and my husband arriving home safe.
But like a wife at her loom, I'll sit in my window,

against light's massive argument with dark,
picking at the threads, singing
to the one who grips the far end.

What We Flash at the Darkness

after Charles Wright

I'm talking about a room overlooking a bay,
mountains in the distance, the stillness.

I'm talking about the hush of lace curtains,
the lift and fall.

I'm talking about the morning sun pouring in.
On the table, a dish of peaches, a jar of pink peonies.

About sheets in a heap on the white-washed floor,
your cheek touched by a tremor of light.

About our mouths still open in wonder,
my fingers pressed to your lips. Salt, a trace of ash.

Relics

Easter again and a small rain falls,
and because of her stroke-robbed memory
my grandmother can't remember the language
of prayers, their complicated invocations.
She doesn't recognize the Son of God
exalted to a spot on the wall above her bed.
Nor her plaster St. Jude, patron of lost causes,
St. Francis opening his arms in the yard.
At the window, she watches clouds assembling,
three crows on a limb talking in tongues.
This morning, still dark with early spring,
there's no sign that anything rises out of itself.
Only I go back, remembering her life of small deaths
and refusals, her marrying at seventeen a man
who belonged all these years, except on paper,
to other women. Because of God
she wouldn't divorce him. Now she's lost God, too.
She sits at the window, succored, as if in exchange
she's been gifted with this world's visibility.
Let Us Pray the priest for the shut-ins whispers,
but her rosary, tangled beads, collects dust,
the only sound the wind retelling its story.
In my own godlessness, I want to squelch
the terror of lost memory,
not utter a prayer I don't know how to make.
For her sake, I hope her God has been listening,

another way of saying, perhaps, *Have mercy.*
The priest lifts the Host to her lips
but she glances away from the window,
her mouth clamped shut.
To her it's sleight-of-hand, nothing more
than a moon ascending.

Another Version

From a coffee shop's sidewalk table,
I watch a nursing home's entrance.
Outings over, the elderly are dropped
like afterhour deposits at the Drive-Thru window.
Flash of walker and wheelchair, mouthed promises
of *next time, next time*, of, perhaps, the child
who routinely disappears, hates how his grandma smells,
how her spidery hands, like a drunk's for a bottle,
grab him each time he tries slipping past.
How quickly the families pull back
into traffic, into their complicated lives.

                                    In this version,
I've made the woman no one comes to see
childless, eighty. Naturally
she sits in the least-lit room, at the greatest remove
from this May afternoon's merger
of green branch and forget-me-not blue,
her only company books off-duty nurses read aloud
and a man's pocket watch that long ago ceased
marking, with any accuracy, time.
In old photographs, how remarkably
her features resemble mine.
She's still grateful for the few cards at Christmas
and from a distant nephew's daughter another robe or cardigan,
how the wrapping, over all those miles,
still intact, survives.

But oh, to have back
these shifts of light maples make
on a table, a lazy weekend afternoon spread
like a banquet. Some days, the smallest
sound, a faintest whiff, and her head still lifts,
a glimmer in her eyes' glaucous blue.
As though she were waiting for me
to finish my coffee, pick up this bouquet
of heady freesias, fleshy rubrum lilies, which I gave
every impression to the store clerk
were for me.

When More Compelling Thought Seems Required

These late afternoons of long shadows,
of mournful wind in the eaves, tempt me
to look back, consider all the time I squandered
over breakfast, gazing out at the garden,
a calamity of grackles in the oaks.
And because a shaft of fading sunlight
finds the blue bowl of tangerines on the counter,
more compelling thought seems required,
reassessment of the hours.
If I'm not careful, if I allow
the chilled Chardonnay to beckon too early,
dissipated hours might accrue
to days misspent and men I should have said no to.
I heat the coffee kettle instead, whistle
to the dog for a walk. In the autumnal light
we get no farther than the yard where I rescue
late tomatoes from an incipient frost.
Other times like this, I often consult
Escoffier, attempt redemption
with a complicated *vol au vent*.
But I'm not in the mood to cook.
Instead, inside, I put on some music—Beethoven's
late quartets— and soon, from a favorite chair
facing west, I'm considering my heart's
contrapuntal knock, its perfect
da-dum-da-dumming iambs.

The dog's head is in my lap,
and just before nightfall, how I love
the brief flare of numinous light,
its almost saving grace.

III

Meanwhile

Jeremy Point

*"...the outermost of the outermost reaches, a narrow
sandspit submerged except at lowest tides."*
       —A Cape Cod National Seashore sign

After Wellfleet's certainties of buildings and harbor,
after the tenuous islands, the rivering salt marsh,
Great Beach Hill, scrub oak and pitch pine,
after glacial drift, tumbled beach glass,
a horseshoe crab's armored carapace—
at last the last of the sandspits.
I'm beyond the tidal flats, the gulls'
shattered remnants, beyond all vegetation.
No sails, no trawlers, just a lifting tern,
a few offshore feeding brant. Abstracted,
this landscape of shimmering elemental planes
is all mine, temporarily.
At the outset I was warned of the flood tide's
daily reclamation, its hourglass turn
disguised as a sheet of brilliance. Water
already laps some bird's scribblings in the sand.
This dialogue of sea and land is endless,
a mercurial negotiation. And my undoing
if, immobilized by its beauty, I don't go back.
Will can't halt the tide's advance. Nor longing.
I've come so far. Never again this path
with these specific tracks: mine, recognizable.

And how their simple unswerving line
is really a subtle elongated arc.
In the journey out, I'd been so certain
it was straight.

Walking the Dog

By instinct alone the opossum stiffens.
I'm supposed to believe
it's nothing but a carcass,
that its white picketed teeth
serve no further purpose,
nor the snout, the prehensile tail.
Even its eyes refuse to focus.
But only the dog is fooled.
Tomorrow there'll be a wiser dog, a quicker cat.
There's nothing that says the opossum will live
through this night, through the next hour.
I could tell it everything
is no longer possible. I could tell it
I will not see everything before I die.
Not just cities, whole continents missed,
glaciers and mountains, someone else's air
I might've breathed into my lungs.
Poor opossum. On this night
thick with constellations I'm still learning to name,
all it can do is amble back to its stump
until again it must, to stay alive, play dead.

Elegy for J.

Today when the clouds refused to remain clouds,
when cicadas ceased their seventeen-year slumber
at the exact moment she put her daughter down
for a nap, and after she'd finished
peeling an apple and it lay cupped in her palm
and she looked down not certain
how it got there, today, an ordinary day,
when every hair on her head fell in love
with gravity and she came across the blue bandana
he wore when his fell out,
when the wind from some distant place failed
to fill his shoes, when for an entire hour she did
nothing but watch a shadow climb the side of the house,
disappear over the roof, today,
when the man next door in rubber flip-flops drove
to the mini-mart, scratched a single Lotto ticket
with a borrowed dime and won the $50,000 Jackpot,
and the wind blew up in quick, sudden swirls
reminding her of autumn when leaves look
like they want to work their way back to trees,
today, when in that white-tiled health care office,
another elbow was uncrooked for a nurse,
when her daughter fell off her Big Wheel
and she asked Where does it hurt? but wished
she could point at herself, answer,
Here and here and here,

when she sent her son to buy zucchini
and he came home with cucumber instead
and so she sent him back for salmon steaks
which cost $10.98 and required a chilled Trebbiano
which, if she'd known, she would've invited a guest,
today, when her body replaced perfectly
its million cells that die every twenty-four hours
and she thought nothing about it
but couldn't remember if immunity has one m or two,
when from the porch she saw a shooting star, worried
if there were enough to spare,
wondered why the constellations never change,
why, for example, Pegasus never loses a hoof
or Orion a piece of his bow,
she remembered what her brother once said:
How can you lose yourself in the story
if all you think about is the end?

Meanwhile

All morning, relaxing into details
of housework, of closing the cottage, I'm quietly one
with a sunlit room, its bits of dust.

Until, for no particular reason—
or, rather, for how the asters won't come again
but the vase is constant to the table,

and the book with its spattered pages
can't be read again for the first time but is faithful
to the shelf where sunlight angles—

I remember "See you next summer,"
how we all said it last night at season's end,
old friends embracing, even the reticent men,

and we reminisced, resurrecting
decades of picnics on the barrens,
skiffs doused by spray heading for Eagle Island.

We showed scant interest in the sky's
consolation of stars flaring and persisting,
or how the tide nudged in and out,

each wave overlaid by another, embossed

like fish scales, but ephemeral.
"Next summer," we promised.

Meanwhile, on this table by the window,
there's a wren's nest and a bare-chambered shell
where something inside once hungered.

Further off, the Camden Hills are explicit,
not one reduced to a rock
small enough to carry in my pocket.

The Comfort in Named Things

Say auk, not duck.
Say alcid, black guillemot.
To granite ledge, add
glacial, magma, volcanic.
Specify cove with Cat,
Burnt, or Crockett.
Like the map, make islands
Moose, Hardhead, Little Pickering.
Point, if you must,
if you can't connect Ursa,
Major or Minor, or Orion.
Alone in a rented cottage on the shore,
rename love. Say
Bob, Ben, Christina, Michael.
Learn ebb and flow, neap and flood.
If necessary, invent a word
for waves that don't hesitate
in their slap and slide,
for the waning moon
that doesn't tremble.

Just When

Just when I think I could live here year-round,
I sit down to brunch with a native
who wears a torn T-shirt and plastic flip-flops,
who speaks much louder than she should,
as though for years she's had to shout
above a gillnetter's thumping diesel.
As it turns out, she cares for her mother,
ninety-six, whose hearing is gone,
who's never known a life off-island.

Just when I think, tying up to Town Dock,
I might be absorbed into the ebb and flow,
mistaken, perhaps, for a Dow or an Eaton, I use
boat instead of *trawler*, *cormorant* rather than *shag*.
Driving the Cross Road, I round a curve and flinch
at another listing trailer, more rusted cars on blocks.
Or, afternoons, I look up, see rubber-booted clammers
bent to their work on the flats, more kin
to lesser yellow legs, black-bellied plovers
than to me on the deck with a book.

Just because I can read the tidal charts,
can, with some accomplishment, swim,
what do I know of the cold Labrador current,
what it takes to survive an island winter, marooned
when the Thorofare freezes over?

From a shore-front summer cottage, the horizon
looks limitless, a perspective not shared,
I'm to believe, by the teenagers at Sparky's,
fourth-generation lobstermen, daughters of women
who pick crab in their kitchens.

Come September, I'll again pack my wagon,
eddy into the stream of traffic on the causeway.
Racked with our ten-speeds and kayaks,
we drive back to our jobs governed
by custom, convenience, the Dow Jones Index.
No one sees us off. But I can imagine it:
as if we were aboard a schooner
putting out from the harbor toward a distant,
tideless skyline where water ends,
where no one rakes, drags or traps—
and the locals, waving from the wharf,
are exuberant. Just when they think
we'll never go, we're gone.

From a Dune above Herring Cove Beach

It's my turn to flatten the spartina grass.
Like others before me, I contemplate the sea,
the rafts of black eiders, and today, a lowering sky,
ash-colored swells from a composition by Whistler.

I want to follow a wave all the way in
but I keep getting lost in the troughs,
in the churning gravity set in action
somewhere off the Atlantic shelf.

And such dizzying permutations:
each form similar, no two identical,
like snowflakes, sand grains,
our whorled thumbs.

Out in the watery cleats,
one bristling scroll at last unwinds,
gathers momentum. It's a mighty specimen.
With a storm behind it, this one

could pull from the bottom a half-ton hull,
dump it on the beach like a bottle.
Faithful as Penelope, I mean to stay
with my wave to shore, but when I blink

at a passing gull's shadow, it's lost

to any of many spumy crashes, disappears
into evanescing froth. Beneath the sand,
there are no recirculating pumps.

Come September, no salted wave
will pool around an inland garden's asters.
From this height, it seems appropriate then
to say a few words about my roller,

how it spawned so many wavelets,
how this stretch of coastline
wouldn't be the same without it.
And consider the journey:

how it summered in Fiji,
survived the Cape of Good Hope in foul weather,
surfed the Gulf Stream, stirring
whatever it touched.

How, at the final moments,
it tried to take everything with it
in that raking hiss, that *yes, yes*
of shells, stones sucked from their sockets.

My Mind's Eye Opens Before the Light Gets Up

after Philip Booth

The math I refigure in the dark still comes up short—
my roof will have to hold another year, the peeling clapboard

won't get paint. I count instead the pounds
I aim to lose, the miles I'll have to run to do it.

Just what will I serve to this weekend's guests—
a carnivore, three vegetarians, two dieters

sworn off sugars and carbs? Eyes shut,
I replant the garden: peas not leeks, more squash, no beets.

This season, how many quarts of blueberries did I fail
to freeze? On the coverlet, my hand tells my head

we've moved toward frost, to that one day
white-throats in the thickets know to leave, but I can't say

how many minutes of light each day has already dropped.
I preview winter's average snowfall,

snapped power lines, a depleted cord of hardwood,
replay my tumble down the cellar steps last December,

the number of bones I might've broken.
Once when money was a bigger part of the equation,

a rich man asked me to marry. I no longer keep track
of other roads not taken, don't enumerate

the people lost to my carelessness, neglect.
Still, before the light gets up, I'm moving

from aimless drift and inventory into the dangerous
territory of reconsideration, of the impossible parity

between joy and satisfaction, sorrow and regret.
Soon now, the sun will report the morning's weather

I have no say in. With another day,
another chance to balance the books, only a fool wouldn't be

grateful beyond measure.

Salt Marsh

Here, love, on the salt marsh
is where we ought to live,
build a last house. Let's dwell
among these undulant horizontals,
these lucent pools, small grassy islands
combed by white egrets.
I want to add my obbligato
to the white-throated sparrow's
five-note pleading. I want to stay
among these dusky sedges and plums,
this pointillist stammering of yellow-eyed asters.
Let's reside with these endless repetitions,
each tidal transit a confirmation
the cosmos is still intact. Think of how
each light-shot room would shine.
Imagine the pitch pines, their broomy music.
I mean it: a house
shingled with cedar, a deck we'd ornament
with emptied whelks, limpets,
a few potted lilies. We'd haul over
our blue ladderback chairs, our wicker table,
even that silly calendar of the costumed dogs.
We'd serve chilled wine, pan-seared flounder.
There'd be no need for a manicured lawn.
Think of the shift and flux, the widening
pools and streams disappearing

under a scoured tidal sheet.

Even while we sleep. And how,

with the ebb, it all comes back:

the clam-blistered mudflats, the glittering sand bar,

the marsh grasses' lustrous shiver.

And out on the reach, where intersecting sea and sky

appear as a seamless spill,

the lighthouse, vigilant guardian,

keeps careful watch. In fog, in steely mist,

its blinking beacon warns against,

or, like the stars, the moon, beckons.

Notes

"In the Hospital" is written after Gregory Djanikian's "In the Hospital Room."

"A House-Moving" is written after Marianne Boruch's "House Moving."

Some of the images in stanza five of "The Bisbee Donkeys" derive from William Greenway's "Pit Pony."

"Northern Flicker" is written after "*In Paradisum*" by Thomas Lynch.

"Passage" is written in response to Robert Cording's poem, "Pilgrimage."

The title, "To the Days Lost in August," derives from a line by Philip Booth in "Vermont: Indian Summer."

"From Away" is written after and begins with the same line as Elizabeth Bishop's "Little Exercise."

Some of the images in the final lines of "Refusal" derive from Dorianne Laux's "Graveyard at Hurd's Gulch."

The epigraph of "Last Week a Million Butterflies" refers to the Butterfly Effect in James Gleick's *Chaos*.

The title, "What We Flash at the Darkness," is borrowed from the last line of "Morandi" by Charles Wright.

The first line of "Relics" is from "The Other Side of the River" by Charles Wright.

"Elegy for J" is in memory of Jim Cummins.

The title, "My Mind's Eye Opens Before the Light Gets Up," is borrowed from the opening lines of "Adding It Up" by Philip Booth.

About the Author

Deborah Cummins is the author of a poetry chapbook, *From the Road It Looks Like Paradise.* Her awards include James A. Michener and Donald Barthelme fellowships, the Washington Prize in Fiction, the Headwaters Literary Prize, Illinois Arts Council fellowships and awards, and fellowships from Yaddo, MacDowell, Ragdale, and Virginia Center for the Creative Arts. Now president of the Modern Poetry Association, she has also been an Arts-in-Education artist with the Illinois Arts Council, writer-in-residence at Menil Museum of Art in Houston, Texas, and lecturer at the University of Chicago. She has directed writing workshops at Northwestern University and at Chicago's Museum of Contemporary Art, Terra Museum of American Art, and Newberry Library. She resides with her husband, Bob, in Evanston, Illinois and Deer Isle, Maine.

CPSIA information can be obtained
at www.ICGtesting.com
Printed in the USA
FFOW02n0646090414
4766FF